*for Mickey —
I'm very excited to
have you in my
life now — lets be in
touch —
Art LOVE
Carole
Watanabe
2010
Jerome*

"Carole Rae Watanabe, master painter and colorist, has her own unique language to express the varied cultures and environments she inhabits internationally. Her spontaneity of line and gesture, her intense color palette and her imaginative and mysterious ability to touch people deeply are signature elements of her career."

Sandy Thompson - Executive Director
Center for Comtemporary Art - Santa Fe, New Mexico

Meet Artist and Author
Carole Rae Watanabe

If you have interest in purchasing my
paintings or books or spending a vacation in any of my Art Houses in France
or Mexico, please look at your options
on www.artfully.com
I am always available for commissioned
work and creative brainstorming about
your art needs.

Order my new video:
Create the Artists' Dreamlife
The nitty-gritty of being an artist,
how-to instructions, visual inspirations
and more. www.artfully.com

Carole Rae Watanabe

Layout & Design: Carole Watanabe
Photography: Don Watanabe

LiveArt Editions, Sebastopol CA

©copyright 2008
Printed in China
ISBN 978-1-60725-354-9

Be the Burning Brush

The Ecstatic Marriage of LIFE and ART

FOR

Tobin Yelland, my son, who is the breath
of fresh air under my wings again and
again.

Edith Buckley, my savvy real estate
guide and Mom

Don Watanabe, my amazing Buddha

Table of Contents

Author's Preface

Finding the pulse of creative juice where all expression is born is an extraordinary feeling at any time and in any media and it is your BIRTHRIGHT. We were all artists in kindergarten. This is your survivor's manual to help gain access to the quiet place where deeply personal happiness dwells. Hopefully, these words from my journals will open the art-filled 'Gate of Solace' that I'm attempting to guide you towards and through.

When Art and Life Merge

When I put the thick glistening gold paint on and watch the fine red thread of color migrate from the canvas back to an outstretched bristle of the brush and then see it collide with a tiny mound of blue-violet edging the white lily of the painting, I know and feel why I paint.

It's the squealing in my soul, the physical flood of endorphins, and the slow motion visual magic of mistakes turning towards magnificence. The simple white canvas and paints, generating love from somewhere so unpredictable and sacred, that I simply surrender and paint usually in awe of God. For an artist, god is Creativity. Art is an open gate to the divine.

Acknowledgments

Noelle Oxenhandler, who included me as creative catalyst in her book The Wishing Year, and encouraged me to haul out 40-years worth of my journals and glean from them pivotal stories, inspirations and revelations that helped me create and compile this book.

To buy Noelle's book go to <thewishingyear.com> or <noelleoxenhandler.com>

Wat, my Buddha life mate who has photographed the painted pages of this book while they were still dripping wet and kept up with the whirlwind of my process with wisdom and grace.

Lorelei Brede, my assistant who has taken my writings covered with sticky notes, arrows, added scraps and sculpted them into a readable form.

Salli Rasberry and I wrote The Art of Dying which is about living your life in a vibrant, brave way using the awareness of death to render one's-self more awake and engaged. I've borrowed some of the passages as they are the parent words to this book. Thank you Raz.

Sara Spaulding Phillips, another close friend and power-house of a woman has written a 'sister' book called Journey Book to Self Discovery. Sara demonstrates practical projects and steps to take when you need an inspiring art coach to spur you on in your Art life.

To buy Sara's book go to <saraspauldingphillips.com>

Chapter
One

To Be An Artist

Be

The Burning Brush

To be an Artist

is the most personally empowering job you can engage in. You are the keeper of the intensely powerful gift of touching the world's soul. You can bring beauty and peace to huge segments of our world and even succeed visibly. You and only you are in charge of what you create, how often you show up, and where you choose to go in a world filled with options. And it follows that your soul needs nurturing, supporting, loving and - depending on the size of your ego - lots of shows and checks arriving to keep you motivated and fully engaged.

This creative need to live your life and your Art as one ongoing potent process necessitates the marriage of life to your art. It demands a no-fear right brain for creative leaps, a fully functional left brain to keep the business in the black and an immense trust in the creative process and in yourself. It also demands the realization that society is dependent on artists to go to the edges of vision and continuously check the vital pulses of our planet and its people. Out of a humble yearning for clear vision, the artists are the eyes for society. There is nothing else so worthy of my time and life. For me Art is the gate of solace for the makers and viewers alike.

11

The Practice

of being an Artist or any type of creative 'Danger Ranger' is to continually embrace your own personal creative fire. In order to maintain your bodacious momentum, you need to honor and expand the gifts of creativity which you've been given.

Out of this heat emerges the phoenix of new forms, new loves, and a high intention for a more spirited way of living and being.

"I am the Art" becomes your mantra. Say it often until all doubts disappear.

Be the Burning Brush

JUST PAINT, and the necessary fuel for your art fire will grow. When you paint, you are the burning brush, you are no longer on the outside observing. Art leaves nobody out - you are a part of the world's creative juice and force - the tool of the world's spirit. All paintings emerge from the interior caverns of our soul - Art is the unbinding of the love you have stored and re-stored from the powerful images in your heart. All the richness that you have received from the glistening droplet of light in sunrise to the terrifying dreams of your dark side will flood into your own form - your own voice in paint on that white void of the canvas. Your role is to get your minds' voices out of the way and let the swimming-in-the-creative-juice-of-the-universe begin.

It is your birthright - and you have to give yourself permission to step up and claim it. If you don't, the gift only you can give will be forever lost.

In writing these words - I want to provide the stable hand that holds the burning brush. Power words to reflect on and perhaps return to when you need to adjust your attitude - or return to PERSISTENCE.

Art is Love

and persistence is the only practice that brings the incredible energy of love into form. Use your own brush strokes as a magic cape to protect your _heart's_ core from discouragement. When an idea or new direction comes - act on it immediately with all your grace and wisdom. Give art the power of becoming your guide, your God, your home.

Jeanette Winterson says it so well, "A work of art is abundant, spills out, gets drunk, sits up with you all night and forgets to close the curtains, dries your tears, is your friend, offers you a disguise, a difference, a pose. Cut and cut it through and there is still a diamond at the core. Skim the top and it is rich. The inexhaustible energy of art is a transfusion for a worn out world." _from Art Objects_

Here's how _I_ do art, and it will be different for you - First off, I quiet and center myself with some potent words - and I write the words on the studio wall or the raw canvas - Paint it blue if you feel blue, embrace, accept and magnify what's real this moment. It's your power place to be _in_ and to paint _from_. Try to find your soul in this basket of persimmons. Let go of form and paint simply to access and follow what feels good. Paint this blocked energy and heal your deep pain. I am the heart of water - pull from the under-depths to give your ideas form.

A Collaborative
painting by
Art Heaven
Danger
Rangers:

Carole Barlas
Sandy Caughey
Martha Hart
Laura Jorgensen
Bonnie Karlsen
Alice Liff
M.A. Malkemus
Sara Phillips
Susan Proehl
Sandy Rubin
Judy Tilt
Cherry VanGelder
Carole Watanabe

There will be other voices talking to you - like the 1st grade teacher who said, "Art takes talent dear, and some of us just don't have it."

You have to learn that most of the world tries to hide itself in survival mode. Art is scary because it makes visible our truthful longings for a more profound response and language. A painting about personal truth talks to the parts of our psyche that live beyond survival.

So when the words of fear and survival speak - you can thank them and let them go.

They are the enemy to your finding your own voice in paint. Ask them to please take their places in the corner and leave you to create. Yes, 'talk back'!

Grounding with music that speaks deeply to you is another important part of beginning to paint - unplug the phone, and honor your own gift that wants so badly to float up and out onto the paper.

Art is really nothing anyone can teach you. You already have it inside. I can teach you to honor your personal art and light the candles on your art altar - to close your eyes and envision your feelings in form and color - because what we paint comes from a place much deeper than technique, color rules, or correct perspective. FIRST - paint your passion and the way of technical know how will work on perfecting itself. Just paint in all ways - always. Paint the painting 10 times - by the time you finish - all the *should* voices will fall away in exhaustion – like, "I really should learn to make the pond lay flat, I really shouldn't use these vivid colors which aren't in vogue, I really should have learned to draw, I really should be home paying the bills" – Say thanks to these enemy voices and get on with your work.

Being a Creator

of any sort is like tending a fire - and in the process you learn to protect the dry firewood and matches. You learn that nurturing your art soul is about taking on a quality of life that insures creativity. You learn to feed on joy and beauty and light - with a lot of timelessness and contemplation added to the bliss mix. As artists, our job isn't to put our name on the map - it's to explore all the mountains, valleys and rivers - we are the terrain of our own expression. The painting, the dance and the music is our map. It's the way we find our way home.

Chapter

Two

Making Your Living, Making Your Art

As creative beings, we expand our joy and passion if life itself is lived like a scrumptious picnic, complete with all the exotic flavors and colors we can pack into each life experience.

Making your Passion your Right Livlihood

There are thousands of avenues for artists to make their creative ways in our world. Until you've tried twenty of them and thrived on ten, I'd have to say you haven't really explored your options. Hopefully, these life stories will inspire you to continue your art practice and to try some new roads.

Artists who give light must learn to endure the fire, so peel off your inhibitions and dive deep to the molten core. Your rewards will equal time spent at your art job but keeping a time score can easily de-rail you.

'Bear Bones' Art Laws

For emotional and functional survival, be generous to the true-friends who show up through it all.

Do your art 4 to 8 hours a day with rigorous abandon. Mix this with time for marketing and becoming visible.

Take time to refill creative juice, connect with the earth, share love in all forms, be with interesting artists, and take inspirational walks.

Let your excitement be the guide, try new mediums, use your left hand to access your right brain, use only 2 colors for a week, change to 3D clay or vice-versa

Control is not useful in many art forms - art is about opening wide to energy forces we don't see -"go with the flow" means move over negative messages ,out of my way rigid plans, give me space so the creative muse can find room to land and do her magic. Art is something other than you and your ego.

Stand in front of your art altar and ask to be filled with rich rainbow light, let if fill every cell and ooze out through your fingers - play and dance on the bare canvas without a plan. Let art be your instinctual guide - your direct connection to the divine.

Reaching blissful flow-consciousness happens when you practice art like Buddhists practice meditation. Timelessness is - contentment arrives, your mind goes on automatic intuitive pilot and the world dissolves. This is the addictive realm of creators. This is why artists never stop no matter how old.

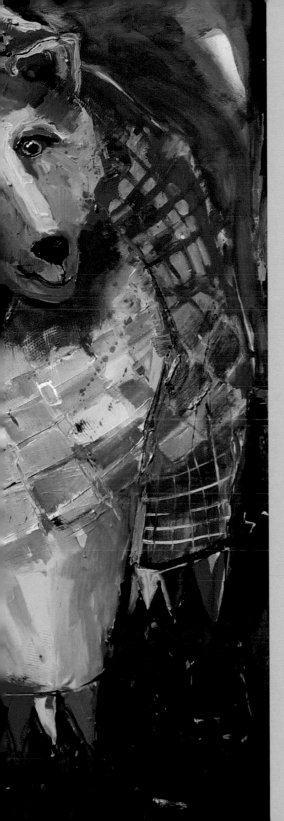

The creative nurturing life demands the art of reinventing yourself and your support system - again and again. It's not about money or fame or about fitting in. It's about listening for clear clues and letting personal creative urges become the guide. Life is so precious and so short. We must keep the flow of new patterns and transitions moving in order to fit into the magic adventure, to feed our souls and give our gifts.

Remember change never happens by thinking or talking.

You can both think and talk or you can change. Change is simply being determined to radically shift your patterns! Sit at a table and begin to write your book - pull out the paints and begin your daily practice of being an artist or practice the bass, start the jazz band, be the musician you've always yearned to be. Change is action. Art your socks off!

When I make major life shift changes, I visualize myself borrowing a used niche from an ancient Buddha and becoming the new spirit in the new shrine I long to inhabit. It helps to create an actual shrine complete with words and symbolic objects to make the direction clear.

Transition times are the times of greatest vulnerability. It's important not to respond or react to the judgments of society and peers. I like to say, "I'm doing a 2-year life experiment and I'll be willing to discuss it when I've gathered more real life experience. Write JUST DO IT and diligently water the root, "To get your fill of flowers and fruit, water the root". Keep your eye on the prize of personal expansion.

Your imagination is a muscle – take it to the art gym daily and use it on everything you do, paint, say, make and feel. If you get bored, try painting collaboratively and surrendering your precious marks to the collective genius of 2 or 3 partners on a canvas. It is the greatest teacher I've found; teaches you that nothing is so sacred it can't be improved.

When you lock into a style or a particular medium and repeat your successes for too long, something inside begins to atrophy. When art starts feeling like a job, you have to cut yourself adrift once again in search of an Art Heaven where a beginners mind is your key to aliveness and re-discovery.

You are the only person on earth who can reclaim your creative energy.

Please do it to help balance the negativity we all experience.

ART
amps up the quality of our lives both
individually and collectively.

Create

your support system and take good care of it. Give art away regularly to auctions that benefit expanding creativity in your community, in art centers and art programs in the schools and neighborhoods.

Have shows regularly anywhere – including your living room or local ice-cream shop and invite your friends.

Don't skimp on time to play music, sing, dance, or cook – whatever gives you satisfaction. Don't be stingy with yourself. Marinate in juicy new input.

WHEN you are in the dumps or recovering from illness or hard patches of any sort, learn to paint your way out to the place where excitement returns. Connecting with your creative center is the road to, "Somewhere Over the Rainbow".

Becoming a Danger Ranger Warrior of Art

Danger Rangers are complete human examples of fine art that is alive. They create individualized worlds based on their intuitive visions. Change and growth are met with an expectation of miracles, and as a result miracles become the natural resources of a Danger Ranger. The Danger Rangers motto is "Dissolve Parameters".

Basically, we are an adult scout troop who earn badges that encourage members to take risks, make major changes, and explore a more potent and dynamic life-style. Our badges are based on the Principles of Neutral Buoyancy: practice playing, let spontaneity lead, be still - breath - let go, choose aliveness now, there are no rules, dive and swim - you are in charge, appreciate the void - listen, do less - be more, listen to your original heart.

Members create the badges they want to achieve and then work on them with support and camaraderie from the group. An example is the Endless Fantasy Badge. Whenever you think of a fantasy - write it down and when the moment arises, make some of them real. Example: be a human center-piece at a banquet with friends. Begin the 'being eaten' fantasy with two assistants bathing you. Next, lie down on a dining table nude and have them cover you with a bouquet of flowers to hide your head, cold cuts covering all your skin, bowls of dips and salads between and around your legs - maybe a huge baked fish down your chest. This is a fantasy that demands complete stillness to pull it off. Your challenge is to remain undiscovered for an hour as your friends nibble at the salami on your thighs.

Choose three fantasies and do them

Photograph an especially interesting one and have the photo printed on a t-shirt. "I am my fantasy" could be written underneath the photo. At parties, pretend to be writing a book about fantasy. Jot down notes of the most incredible fantasies from people you interview and read your book at the next Danger Ranger meeting.

Begin to interchange fantasy with reality and vice-versa. They are equally demanding and exotic games. The world is in desperate need of creative Danger Rangers.

To get more details on how to start your own Danger Ranger Club, go to www.artfully.com

It's hard to say if life takes art for a ride or vice-versa. Whatever it may be, hopefully, your ride will be wild and wonderful. Ye Ha!

HOW I BEGAN

From kindergarten on, painting has been a process of connecting, a way to standout, an urge to have a meaningful, gutsy experience and more fun. When the 5-year olds in school made a pretend store, I was on the floor with a big roll of paper painting the red and white stripped awning. The principal walked me home to tell my parents I was an artist and they should get me lessons. My dad had already made me my own easel at age 3 and we had two family friends who were perfect role models for my creative spirit – Doris, who kept me supplied in abundant paints, paper and clay and Missy Rozelle, a dazzling bon-vivant in huge hats and Parisian outfits who became my surrogate 'Art Grand-Mother'. My life was all about making. My 2nd grade teacher used to lend me to other teachers to paint in front of their class. The kids would say, "Paint a lion or a flamingo", and I would. My art became my identity.

I allowed myself to become very focused-obsessed and in love because, in observing my options, Art seemed like the only thing I wanted to do well. I never grew out of it

BEST OF THE
BAD GIRLS

I've seen people choose to make Art their identity at age 60 as well. All it takes is a deep love of life, the cultivation of perception and the ability to suspend inner and outer judgments. The profound work of an artist is to make one's self deeply happy. There are a zillion directions to explore. In Art College at age 18, I was exploring abstract forms of lichen patterns on graves. My painting teacher wanted me to intellectually explain my symbolism, my message, and my reasons. After 6 months of feeling ridiculed and embarrassed by his judgments during critiques, I stopped painting and changed my major to tapestry weaving.

Little did I know I was learning the most important lesson that could be offered up at any art college, "After giving it your all and not succeeding, make a direction change and continue to create with renewed spunk".

I dug in with intensity and determination. My teacher, Trude Guermonprez, became my beloved mentor and we shared a deep appreciation for each other. She planted valuable seeds in me, "You are on the crest of the wave of the fiber revolution, large corporations will support you if you think and weave on a grand scale." After graduation I chose a 5-year detour down Wilderness Road, where I took baby steps weaving functional items, like purses, pillows and shawls. Trude continued to visit and encouraged me with invitations to talk with her classes on the subject, "You really can make your living as an artist". On my fifth year in the woods, Trude gave me a much needed kick in my art-butt - "You're wasting your talents; life is about more than survival, I'm afraid you've forgotten you are a Fine Artist."

Even now, writing her words brings a flood of tears. She cared about me and didn't want me to get lost in 'strawberry fields forever'. But I'm jumping ahead to the next chapter on incubating my talents and bravery on Wilderness Road.

J'espoir que ma barque chantera

Watanabe

31

Chapter
Three

Wilderness Road Survival Training

Thriving on your chosen handcrafted life brings a miraculous sense of well being.

You would think that living

on the idyllic South fork of the Eel River in the late 60's with the other "flower children" would be pretty serene and simple – "Living with strawberry fields forever". Not so – it was the riskiest, most demanding, labor-intense phase of life that I have ever experienced. The primal tangle of urgent needs – grow your food, bake bread, build a house, create a livelihood in a 2-room cabin; give birth, do diapers by hand, heat with wood or freeze, buy land, create community for survival, train a work-force, fit into a red-necked loggers world, start a pre-school, a food co-op, and the Wilderness Road Weavers – seemed endless. And there were also large doses of exquisite moments and sublime magic in the mix.

The basic structure of the warp threads crossing the weft ϕ became my guiding symbol and mantra for centering as I worked through my five years of Art Boot Camp. I taught my painter-husband Robert to weave and we embarked on the most important lesson for our new life and livelihood, "How to make something out of nothing". We discovered our new magical world while on an art college field trip called the S.P.O.N.G.E. Expedition (Symbol, Projection, Orientation, Nurtured, and Guided Ecologically). We lived on the Northern California Coast Range Preserve of the Nature Conservancy and studied the art and ecology of the amazing Eel River Valley. The 4,000 acre preserve was the most isolated wonderland in California and we decided we had to live there.

To pay for our new life, I invented Camp Unify, a summer camp for Oakland inner-city kids and ran it with 10 of my best artist friends. The Point Foundation and Huey Johnson of the Nature Conservancy gave me a grant and I was off on a wild and wondrous ride for a middle class kid from San Diego. I met two important mentors, Arch Mitchell who offered us a two room cabin on his nearby land in trade for homemade bread weekly and Heath Angelo, an ecological wizard and far-thinking business man who had saved the 4,000 acre preserve from loggers and ended up teaching me everything I needed to know about self sufficiency and the life of those who choose to live on the far edges of society. In fact my #1 Art Law for Danger Rangers had its rigorous test phase during my basic training there.

"Creative juice always provides what's needed."

We ate what we grew, we built a house from a Sunset guide book, I trained apprentices to spin, dye and weave, I founded the Wilderness Road Weavers, we gave birth to Tobin Yelland, we lived on less than $10,000 a year and it was the most important foundation phase I could have had for the 'life-of-an-artist' life style. I was inventing and enduring my own Boot Camp for artists, a trial by fire.

One favorite visual memory, to give you the flavor of my existence, took place on my river front platform built into a circle of six redwoods. There I sat listening to the river with Tobin in his play pen and me spinning rustic wool skeins for my mail order business of natural dyed yarns. Tiger Lilly Jones, my live-in apprentice, was threading the finished skeins onto a rope which stretched across the Eel River to

CAMP
UNIFY 1
1968

NORTHERN
CALIFORNIA
COAST
RANGE
PRESERVE

gently wash them. Dr. Dean Edell's wife was fording the river on her horse to invite us for dinner at their tipi. What an adventure for a middle-class girl from San Diego.

There were also hard times like when we had 67 cents left to our names and were on our way to a fair to sell three months worth of woven goods. By the 2nd day nothing had sold and my pregnant body fainted at the spinning wheel. I decided to throw rocks at the walnut trees and forage my dinner. It worked and the nuts held me until an angel showed up the next day and bought $1500 worth of our wares during the closing hour of the event.

Two years later at the Renaissance Fair in Marin County, California, the owners told me my new tapestries weren't very 'renaissance' looking and I wouldn't be admitted the following season. Luckily Alice Liff (who has since become my Art Mother) showed up and offered me my first solo exhibition of tapestries at Gallery III in Marin County. After a near sell-out opening, I decided it was time to shift gears and move to San Francisco where, hopefully, I would have more time for fine art and less time spent in the arts of survival.

The collage on the next page is by Alice Liff.

A work of art is the soul inhaling the colors of passion, and getting drunk on the vibrations of diffused light. It shelters you when reality translates into bad news stories on the black and white screen. When your body/mind is permeated with pain, it lifts you out of your low bed and rocks you with the angels. Art is the gate of solace that leads workers out of their cubicles and back into the lush layers of leaves, dappled light and hopelessly joyful skies that continue opening to the deeper mysteries of life and death.

Weaving A New Life

Unexpectedly, the true Danger Ranger 'city' phase would challenge a whole new set of skills where the stakes were higher and the risks less obvious. I was now a single mom with a 2 ½ year-old son when I decided to start the first tapestry gallery in San Francisco without a cent to my name.

Here are some words from my journals of that year – 1972:

To truly live your life as Art and Artist demands one's relentless attention to the composition of each moment, each frame of the film with a bigger eye on the whole yet unfinished tapestry. This practice demands every discipline you know because you are definitely on trial here. Your son needs a stable home and you need to succeed at being the nurturer and bread-winner or else you are fired from the life you wanted.

Please art guides, show me clear steps and fast. I need to find a gallery space and be successful enough to buy Tobin and me a home, an anchor, a secure life.

I called on Henry Adams whose wife, Claire Ellen was a weaver, when they were just opening The Galleria Design Center in San Francisco. They decided to let me try my Fiber Gallery in the huge 4-story open atrium where there was room for 40 monumental tapestries on the open-air balconies. They built me a very tastful glass showroom overlooking the atrium. I had my loom there and room to display the limited-edition line of my smaller home sized tapestries. I told them I didn't know if there was a sufficient market to pay a monthly lease fee, so we agreed on a percentage of my sales with an upper limit.

I wove like crazy and called every other weaver I knew to make the three month deadline for the opening of Market Week. On opening night, while the champagne corks exploded, I was still putting on the price tags. An hour later, I took an $18,000 order from a store in Dallas that wanted two of each of my 'for homes' tapestries. On the second day, my total for orders was up to $42,000 and I was telling customers that there would be a 6-week delivery time.

Now I understood the bliss and fear involved with success. By the end of Market Week, I had hired an accountant and someone to run the gallery and had joined the Briar Patch – a hands-on, how-to-run-your-own business organization. I had collected $68,000 in gross sales and was baptized into the 'Dive and Swim' method of becoming a business woman.

When Michael Phillips, founder of the Briar Patch arrived to look at my orders and help guide my plan of action, I had to tape record his advice because half of the words and concepts were foreign to me. As I wove I listened to the recording over and over until I had completed every task and then I'd call for another consultation. Michael Phillips and Salli Rasberry had written The 7 Laws of Money, a book that echoed my beliefs. The first law was, "Do what you love and the money will follow". Michael and I were equally quirky and unusual and ended up as mates. He introduced me to all the wild sides of city life and its amazing characters.

After five years of running Carole Rae Fiber Center Gallery, buying my house and living a good life, I walked into a private showing of my tapestries in a Union Street gallery but after two minutes at the opening I walked back out crying. I felt like my art had lost its creative edge – it all looked predictable and I felt my soul sink to the pit of my stomach.

I was exhausted and needed time out, so Michael and I went to re-group in Japan for a month. My journals are filled with drawings of the amazing new aesthetics, garden designs, the serenity of Buddhism, sitting ZaZen and a new fascination with the process of paper-making known as Washi.

When I got home I gave my business to my wonderful weaver employees and made a shrine for my next phase. The words in the shrine said, "Let your old identity die. You have one year to experiment and rediscover your new art form – if you aren't happy by then, you'll have to get a job at the Post Office".

In no time at all a wealthy patron arrived and wanted to commission a large tapestry. I had to tell her I was no longer weaving and that I had taken the year for creative experimenting. Ouch! Two weeks later my brave, sole patron returned and said, "I'd like to support you and I trust that you will make me something great. Use any media you want and I'll send weekly checks for the next 10 months." I cried and I experimented like a fiend and when I delivered the huge sculptural form in a rented truck she gasped with wide eyes. This was her first encounter with the wall hanging and I was terrified that I'd have to refund her money and her trust. She said, "This is way too powerful for my bedroom. We will clear a wall in the gallery and hang it opposite the marble fireplace."

Art Laws for Danger Rangers:

- Creative juice always provides

- Trade passion for the voice of fear

- Visualize your Dream, work like a fiend while you suspend judgments and make your visions real as in 'real' paintings, 'real' shows, 'real' business

- Focus on building inventory and manifesting visibility (shows, websites, etc.)

- When you hit the wall of NOT NOW – NO WAY, and NEVER AGAIN, refill the spring with more rarefied creative juices. Take a class, make art with your mentor, go to inspiring art exhibits, promise a portrait to a friend and have her pose for you, and invite kids over to paint with you. Put yourself on the line.

- Paint freely and only for your own Joy.

Chapter
Four

Wabi Sabi Japan

*J*apan urged me to hush my mind, quell the noise, discipline my actions, meditate to allow newer creative ideas to surface. Hushed stillness is vital to the creative flow.

hortly after the 'magic'

'Patron event, I went to Japan to study paper making as that was the discovery and outcome of my experimental year. Making paper was a potent and liberating process with buckets of gutsy liquid pulp to be dyed, poured, squirted, embedded and played in. The immediacy compared to tapestry weaving was a wonderful freeing pleasure. It felt like being in kindergarden.

Words from my journal:
I'm learning to make paper with a master paper maker and living with his family. I've spent days pounding the mulberry branches into pulp on a huge granite slab with my wooden mallet and watching the busy workshop in a full-tilt boogie as it turns the pulp into beautiful translucent hand-pulled sheets.

49

When Master Ando-san and his crew leave for the evening, I'm free to do my own work. The next day the workers express a lot of excitement to see the white pulp dyed, put in squeeze bottles and squirted into landscapes and abstracted paper paintings. On the last day of my apprenticeship, they invited participants from the other six paper making workshops and had me demonstrate my new technique amidst lots of Sake drinking and exotic Japanese party foods (my favorite is the fresh water eel sushi from the nearby river). I'm only wearing white now so that everything matches and my head is shaved like the art monk I've become. For several moments the Bliss Level has gotten higher than I think I can contain. It feels like orgasm in my heart without flesh. Where does love live and is it stored inside and waiting? This feels like the creative force of the truth river at flood stage and I know it is these moments that blossom into the world's art masterpieces. It has everything to do with deep feelings brought on by unusual seeing. I'm feeling liberated from the constraints of body. The art spirit is soaring with the colorful flying fish kites blowing in the Japanese winds. I now know I am mainly spirit – change the pattern of thought – remember to be art spirit from here on. Soul and Art spirit thrive on clear light and beauty in all forms. I'm adopting Japanese aesthetics as an important guide. I've been invited to spend next summer at Oomoto; a spiritual organization where art is their religion – founded by matriarchal weavers. There will be 30 artists there from all cultures, studying tea ceremony, calligraphy, Noh dance and Budo with venerated masters. This new training will eventually lead to my founding of the Aprentice Alliance in San Francisco.

From an article I wrote in 1982 for The Crafts Report:

My apprentices have been the most meaningful part of my life

When there are no real separations between your work, your pay-check and your life experiences, you fit my idea of a complete artist. And if you add perfection, care and a sense of timelessness to that process you have my idea of a masterful person. When your life and your art are the same, there is an obvious element of personal integrity, passion and real involvement to the work. The field of work is unimportant compared to the quality of your working experiences. This is the philosophy of life and work that the Apprentice Alliance supports.

The goal of the Apprentice Alliance is to acknowledge people who practice this philosophy and to place apprentices with them. Education by doing and being is a good learning situation for trying out your real aspirations. When you are ready to run your 'ice cream' store, why get side-tracked through business school? Hopefully the Apprentice Alliance would place you in a masterfully run 'ice cream' store where you could learn everything from great recipes to keeping the books and cultivating clientele. The philosophy of the Apprentice Alliance has been slowly evolving since I took on my first apprentice in 1969.

I had lived on a wild life preserve and was always amazed when an apprentice would show up in the middle of nowhere to learn weaving. One searcher showed up in the spring when we were planting the garden. All of her possessions were tied to her Volkswagen and she was ready for the complete course. She got out of the car, picked up a hoe and began her three-year stay.

Since then I've taught fifty-six apprentices and have learned to appreciate my relationships with these people as <u>the most meaningful part of my life as an artist.</u>

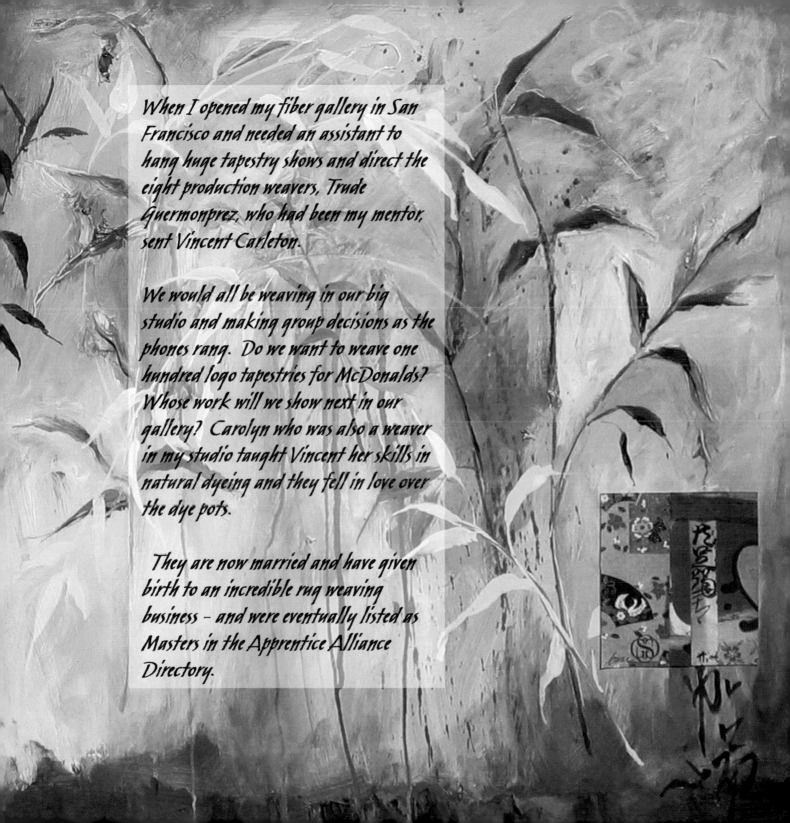

When I opened my fiber gallery in San Francisco and needed an assistant to hang huge tapestry shows and direct the eight production weavers, Trude Guermonprez, who had been my mentor, sent Vincent Carleton.

We would all be weaving in our big studio and making group decisions as the phones rang. Do we want to weave one hundred logo tapestries for McDonalds? Whose work will we show next in our gallery? Carolyn who was also a weaver in my studio taught Vincent her skills in natural dyeing and they fell in love over the dye pots.

They are now married and have given birth to an incredible rug weaving business – and were eventually listed as Masters in the Apprentice Alliance Directory.

Marriage to Myself

The times spent each summer learning the Japanese language and art forms have made me yearn for a more centered, less "wild woman on the loose", type of reality. A new level of refinement is taking hold. The orderliness is so soothing to me emotionally that I'm beginning to crave simple living – not just in my Kyoto garden vacation house but throughout my whole life.

I'M ADMITTING THAT I'M READY FOR A BIG TIME CHANGE

I know I have to make a "must do" list while I'm sitting here in the calm floating world – otherwise, when I return the old life will rush in and drown my new wishes. Here goes – I am making a commitment to change

Liquidate my 2-story house and save only my 100 hundred favorite items that are necessary for life. My art studio is separate and exempt.

Find a solid-rock mate who will give me and Tobin unconditional love.

Have a 'marriage to myself', as I no longer fear that a husband can diminish my freedom, my joy or my independent spirit in any way.

My Marriage Vows to Myself:

I will find and marry a monogomous mate
I want someone who is my equal and who treats <u>me</u> as his equal
I want a rock solid role model for my son
I have one year to find my mate and simplify my life

Upon returning to San Francisco, I gave a 'simple living' party where all my friends came and liberated me from everything material that wasn't essential. I knew I could always re-visit my collections in their homes. Next, I rented a small house on Telegraph Hill, gutted it and turned it into the most exquisite little tea house, complete with tatami mats, shoji screens and a Japanese bath with wooden stools for washing and a drain in the tiled floor so you could luxuriate in water everywhere. I moved in with my 100 favorite items and my 11 year-old son. My previous 2 story house and the complicated life-style I had worked so hard to win had had its day. I rented it out.

I felt it was essential to get the support of friends in my radical-simplification goal and also in my determination to find a solid mate. I printed up a card that told my intentions to every man I met. This was a serious goal with no time to waste on unavailable prospects. I had one year to manifest 'Magic Man'.

The marriage to myself ritual was vital so friends could help me find my mate and hold me to my vows of a simple, monogamous, stable, new-phase of life. On the 11th month I was introduced to Wat (now my husband for the last 25 years) by Thekla who had just moved from Santa Barbara and shared studio space with

me. It was the perfect arranged marriage. He embodied everything about Japanese culture I had come to crave: order, wisdom, competency, care to details and aesthetically he was perfect in the tea house. We were married a year later and have thrived in our union.

Of course, when I wanted to show him my view of Japan, he said he'd rather go to France – and so we were on to the next phase. Japan had been internalized and had helped me go deeper in my own personal development. Japan showed me how to pare down and build the vital foundation for my new self image of the 'detached palace'.

Before returning from Japan, I had watched David Kidd's and Morimoto's ancient detached palace being dismantled for relocation to another property. It seemed they owned the house but not the land. The 300-year old structural timbers were hand carved, massive, and gorgeous and all had structural notching for re-assembly. The walls were woven bamboo and mud, with paper for the shoji doors which were easily removed, letting in huge slanting rays of light. David and his partner, Morimoto-san are the exporters of Japanese arts to Tiffany's. Their aesthetics, collections and possessions are exquisite. I had dined in their intact living museum and the majesty of it all took my breath away.

As my camera clicked incessantly, the raw bones of the palace had me totally mesmerized with their sensuous surrender. Crying, not a few tears for beauty in downfall, but hard deep sobbing, I'm saw my unadorned self image there. Artists feel things deeply – a blessing when they listen. I hear the small warning voice, "Carole, you need your walls, windows and doors die, and move your core-self to higher grounds". You've proven your competency as single business woman and mom and now you need to create your solid family foundation. You need to become the homeland that is truly yours for life. Now thirty years later as I read my journal pages, the big 'Ah Hah' light goes on. The lesson of Japan was, "Be the graceful detached palace and move freely among the cultures knowing you have internalized the massive foundation necessary for grounded security".

The day after I met Wat, my future mate, we were walking past ntique shop and both fell in love with an ancient Japanese temple-shrine. We bought it fifty-fifty with the agreement that he could keep it six months and I could keep it six months. My conscious mind didn't realize it was our symbolic, "Detached Palace", and it would have the honored place in many homes we were yet to build. It took 30 years of process and unearthing my journals to appreciate how miraculous our life stories can be when we are listening, responding and intuitively creating LiveArt.

Chapter

Five

Taking Risks
In The Safety Of
Your Own Canvas

Taking Risks demands that you die into Aliveness.

You have to die into the depths of your love and passion to access the divine creative source. More than any other factor, the willingness to risk will determine your ability to find passion. Passion is the springboard from which art evolves. Risk means switching the button in your head that says, "No I can't" to "Yes I can". The power of changing your attitude to embrace change cannot be overstated. Sometimes the practice of art making demands you <u>let go of</u>: lots of time spent at the easel, expensive paints used and coveting your favorite passages of colors in order to change a ho-hum work into a vibrant magnificent work. Chaos, death and re-birth are the key.

Every risk you take

puts you more in charge of your life. Soon you will be experiencing your life and Art as an adventure instead of a field of landmines that have to be navigated.

One secret to mastering the art of risk taking is to take on smaller challenges first before you attempt a major one. Make it the smallest risk you can take and still feel that you have been challenged. From success with small risks comes confidence. Be sure to acknowledge the tiniest of baby steps. Self-acknowledgement will turn your baby steps into confident strides. You've got to plunge into the fire, slashing and burning with big energetic brushes and then have the self trust to know you'll pull it back out of the ashes in its powerful newly created form. After doing this destroy-in-order-to-truly-create – way of working, you'll find it easier and easier to enter into chaos for the prize waiting at the end.

When you change your attitude towards life or Art, seemingly insurmountable obstacles can be mastered, and you begin to take charge of your life and gain the needed confidence to proceed in directions that lead to self mastery.

In addition to fearing what others think, you must also battle the cultural bias against risk. Risk involves both mistakes and successes. We learn very early that it's not okay to make mistakes, that right answers are good and incorrect answers are bad. You've probably learned, along with the rest of us, to keep your mistakes to a minimum by resisting change and avoiding risk. Anytime we try something new, we risk failure and chaos. Unfortunately, this stops us from enjoying valuable learning and living experiences. The problem is that most people consider success and failure as opposites, not as products of the same process. If you can change your mind's process and experience life more as a journey, then you can progress towards your goal and free yourself and move ahead without fear. An experience or event only becomes a failure if 'you' decide it is a failure. Have you ever noticed that the painting with 3 unfinished paintings underneath it is the one with the richest surface and most soul? It's the one that usually sells first because it was built on failures that you learned from and persisted beyond the, "I can't" mode. 65

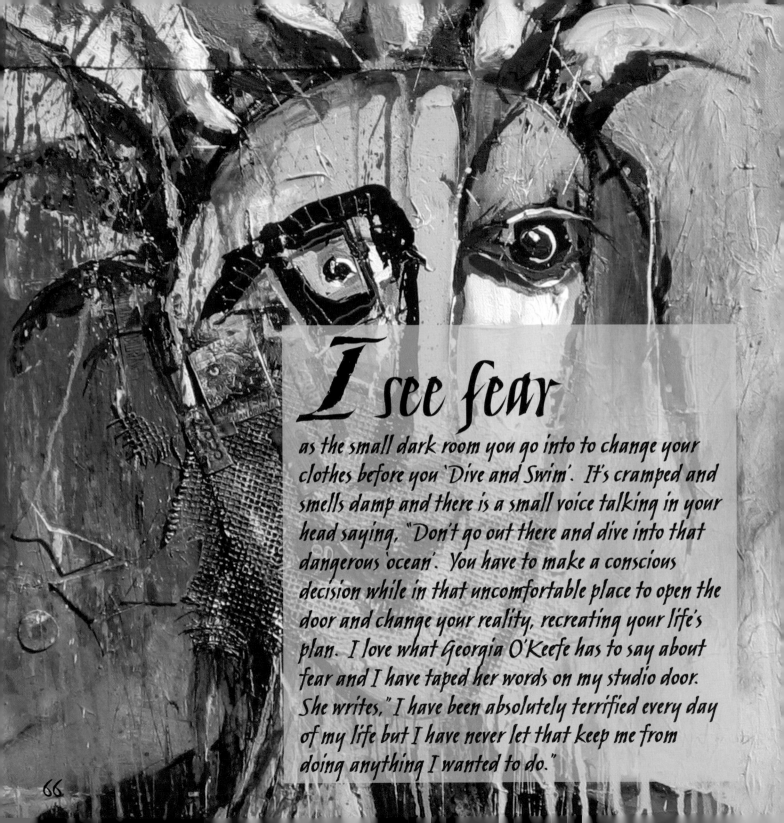

I see fear

as the small dark room you go into to change your clothes before you 'Dive and Swim'. It's cramped and smells damp and there is a small voice talking in your head saying, "Don't go out there and dive into that dangerous 'ocean'. You have to make a conscious decision while in that uncomfortable place to open the door and change your reality, recreating your life's plan. I love what Georgia O'Keefe has to say about fear and I have taped her words on my studio door. She writes," I have been absolutely terrified every day of my life but I have never let that keep me from doing anything I wanted to do."

Live your art

Plant the seeds of your dreams all the time and put no time limits on their blooming. And while your art evolves, be sure to invest chunks of your income in real estate. Buy anything, anywhere you can afford, and rent it out or live in it. Learning to create financial security and an ongoing stable income is _extremely_ important for us creators. Since we can't assume we will have steady cash flow or health and retirement plans, we need to build those things into our life style process. This is not an idea you'll learn at any Art college. The reason your teachers are not out there making their living as artists, is because they never learned to create the steady support and security gained from real estate. My savvy mom, Edith, was frugal and invested in small houses that needed beautifying. As a kid, I helped paint, tile and transform many homes that became rentals. The profits helped my sister and me to advantages that others with blue-collar dads never enjoyed. We had a summer beach house, art, music and dance lessons, yearly vacations, a sailboat at the yacht club and by the time we were in high school, a beautiful home in the nicest neighborhood in San Diego.

Entrepreneurship and creativity are soul mates and totally dependent on each other for keeping body and soul on an even financial keel.

Chapter Six

The Feast
of France

When I want to expand my creative headquarters – like paint in France or Mexico – I immediately ask, "How will my art habit pay for this? Can I give workshops or incorporate a gallery into the mix? Will I profit from using this as a vacation rental?" All creative ventures must generate positive cash flow and allow you the freedom to create without worrying about the bottom line. But then, this is a topic for another book.

Since childhood, I have written journals and stored them, never reading them until I needed quotes for writing this book. I was amazed to see that one quarter of the pages were business plans, from how to market hand-made paper cards to organizing eight weavers and running the first San Francisco Fiber gallery, to founding the Apprentice Alliance, the Danger Rangers and to establishing 'art hide-outs' in various cultures.

The bottom line is that you need to develop ALL of your abilities, to take leaps not only on the art canvas but on the bigger canvas of your life. Art making and Art marketing are governed by similar inner instincts which boil down to work hard and come at the goal from all angles until you succeed. For real art to happen, art has to be in bed with the entrepreneur, or those baby seeds of your dreams will never be born and develop into the masterpieces we are all waiting to behold.

France

is my favorite playground so far. It came about because I thought I was going to die from Lyme disease. My husband and I were building our dream house on twenty wilderness acres in California when I contracted the disease. After putting all of our money and four years of our lives into creating our home, we had to leave it because I was too ill to live in the midst of wildlife. We moved to town. After a time of not being able to talk or move my body, I realized that if I died before I achieved my childhood dream of painting in France, I'd be really disappointed. When I could pick up a crayon, I wrote 'paint in France' on my bedroom wall.

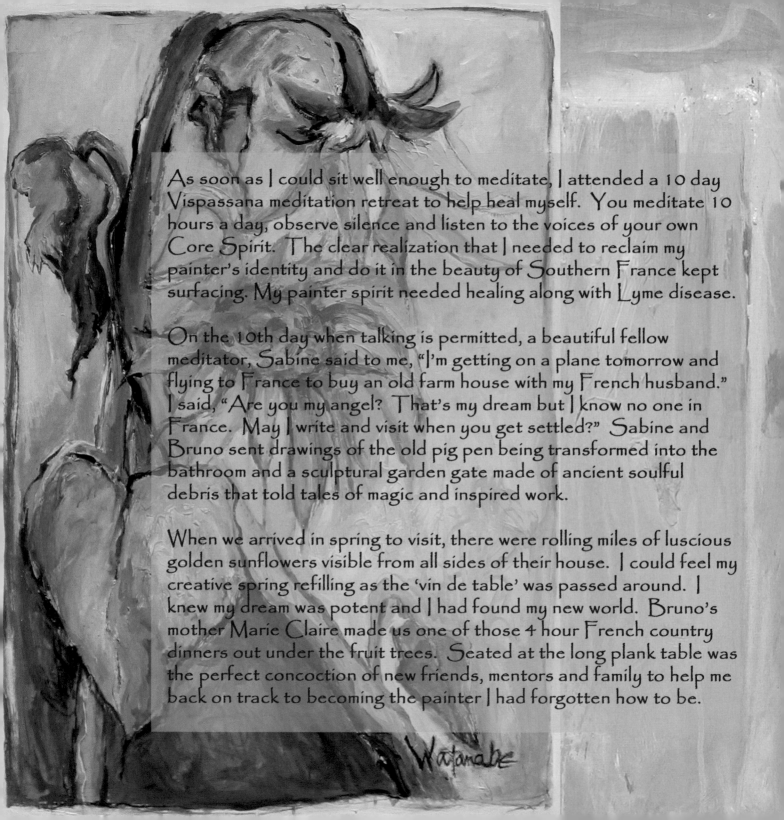

As soon as I could sit well enough to meditate, I attended a 10 day Vispassana meditation retreat to help heal myself. You meditate 10 hours a day, observe silence and listen to the voices of your own Core Spirit. The clear realization that I needed to reclaim my painter's identity and do it in the beauty of Southern France kept surfacing. My painter spirit needed healing along with Lyme disease.

On the 10th day when talking is permitted, a beautiful fellow meditator, Sabine said to me, "I'm getting on a plane tomorrow and flying to France to buy an old farm house with my French husband." I said, "Are you my angel? That's my dream but I know no one in France. May I write and visit when you get settled?" Sabine and Bruno sent drawings of the old pig pen being transformed into the bathroom and a sculptural garden gate made of ancient soulful debris that told tales of magic and inspired work.

When we arrived in spring to visit, there were rolling miles of luscious golden sunflowers visible from all sides of their house. I could feel my creative spring refilling as the 'vin de table' was passed around. I knew my dream was potent and I had found my new world. Bruno's mother Marie Claire made us one of those 4 hour French country dinners out under the fruit trees. Seated at the long plank table was the perfect concoction of new friends, mentors and family to help me back on track to becoming the painter I had forgotten how to be.

Watanabe

Ron Arthaud allowed me to paint 'plein-aire' with him. His passion for the land and light was totally inspiring. There were no intellectual words or judgments – just feeling the amazing beauty and putting it onto canvas. I was in complete awe of his clear truthful work. He invited me to join him at a 2 day painting contest in the medieval village of Soreze. I hadn't painted in years and was terrified, especially when I heard that the villagers judged and awarded prizes at the end. I said no because I was terrified of judgments in any form. The day before the contest I sat by a stream in Soreze and painted an angel. Then words written in patterns began appearing on her robe like:

Reclaim your dream like a warrior
Demonstrate your courage not your fear
Become immune to good and bad words of judgment from everyone from now on
Be the painter who was born to paint
Embrace your life's legend NOW
When you die – die alive

So my psyche and I took courage and said YES to the contest. Sitting and painting for 2 days allowed me to fall completely in love with the cobblestones and bells ringing and smells from baking pan aux raisin and the villagers who stopped, greeted me and brought me lemonade.

THE FEAST THAT IS FRANCE

Paint the light

Ron Arthaud called this a quick sketch. His ability to capture the essence of whatever he saw in such powerful minimal gestures held me in total awe. It was a spring day in the French countryside at a friend's farm and I was feeling very blessed in my "Lucky Duck" hat to be painting with Ron, an angel of a mentor.

Journal Entry:

My whole spirit is expanding to fill the gorgeous old bell tower I'm painting. There is a resonance with this new world that is singing like Maria Callas in my gut – just belting out the Bliss.

I suppose Art and Love are so intertwined for me that I've come to depend on the flow and joy of creative actions like many depend on food. I'm not painting a picture, I'm painting myself onto a canvas filled with new language, new views, new life. In these clearest moments, I know that we are the Art. If I live my life like I paint a painting, my life will be enough.

If I paint my paintings like I live my life, I will return to that state of quiet unconscious primal response where every surface becomes part of an ongoing life's work, every relationship a precious icon. From now on it won't be about what I paint but about the quality of the moments when I'm swimming in the sea of ultramarine bleu or naples yellow. I want to be lost in rich gobs of color. I want to be lost here on this new stage of France where I don't need any protective walls against ugliness. Soreze is like a postcard with downright gorgeous views in all directions. I can go on a lifetime visual vacation here. LiveArt is how these people live. No McDonald's, no over-population, just simple beauty and taking time with what matters: family, friends and of course, the French national religion of food.

L'Art

Spend 10 days at one of Carole and Don Watanabe's art workshops in Soreze, France, and you too will get blissed-out on art.

Above left: Carole Watanabe welcomes vacationers to Art Heaven (L'Art Vivant). Below left: A fountain in the center of Soreze serves as inspiration for a painting by Carole entitled "Crossroads in Soreze." Left center: Students picnic at Lac St. Ferreol. Center: One of eight art-inspired bedrooms at Art Heaven, this one with a van Gogh theme.

Vivant

BY JULIE MACDONALD • *ABN Editor-in Chief*

All she wanted was to paint.

The simple wish of most artists, but one that unfortunately leaves many financially starving and ultimately burnt-out. This was not about to happen to Carole Rae Watanabe. She was going to create an environment that would allow her to "bliss out on art" and pay the bills.

Watanabe, along with her husband Don, created Global Live Art, a company they run from their hometown of Sebastopol, Calif., providing painting workshop vacations around the world. "We just want to be in our favorite places in the world doing art," Carole said as she ran down the list of current and future destinations of art workshops for anyone at any skill level: Soreze, France; Kuai, Hawaii; Bali; and Puerto Viarta, Mexico, to name a few.

The dream unfolded in Soreze, France, where the Watanabe's bought, gutted and built a home and workshop they call Art Heaven or *L'Art Vivant*. In its sixth summer, Art Heaven transforms Soreze, a 400-year-old medieval town in southeastern France, into a destination for vacationers each summer and fall who seek out the workshops for an alternative retreat.

The five two-week sessions are full with 13 students, who, in an intimate very-French setting, learn how to paint with a hidden agenda—to untangle one's spirit and unleash the inner self. Students may hear Carole encourage them to "feed your soul" and "paint your passion" in settings that enforce the message: an open-air market where cheeses, fruits, breads and live poultry are bartered and sold; at Lac St. Ferreol, where a day of painting ends with a catered picnic and live chamber music; a day in the French countryside painting "A Feast for the Senses," a table laden with artichokes, baguettes, quail eggs, *fromage* (cheese) and more, which later becomes the groups lunchtime feast.

Inside Art Heaven, a bed-and-breakfast-type accommodation, students are nurtured further by the in-house chef, a private gallery and eight bedrooms that honor renowned artists, including Matisse, van Gogh, Chagall and Bonnard. A nearby art studio gives students 24-hour access to their paints and canvases.

Awakenings

Painting in France was always a dream of Carole's, which became a reality after her battle with Lyme Disease—Carole's wake-up call. "From now on, I am only doing my dreams," she said revealing how the disease was a link in a chain of events in Carole's life that forced her to continually reinvent herself. "Every time you reinvent yourself," she discovered, "you have to reinvent your marketplace." This, she has done.

The locals in Soreze have become her collectors and her students are friends, friends of friends and sometimes perfect strangers who have seen one of the many articles printed about this special place in the south of France. Thriving on change, Carole is planning a global expansion of her business, opening workshops in—you guessed it—places where the Watanabe's dream of spending time. They are networking with friends around the world planning new art retreats for 2000 and beyond. The Watanabe's are also expanding their client base from individual students to group retreats, with the hopes of adding corporate clients, welcoming even art-market types to reinfused their souls with art.

"We're into creating our own happiness," Carole said. "Besides, I hate the concept of becoming famous when you're dead." And so, alive and well, Carole will continue to paint an example of living one's dream into reality. **ABN**

For information on Global Live Art, call (707) 823-9663, write to 736 Pine Crest Ave., Sebastopol, Calif., 95472 or visit www.artfully.com.

I connected in meaningful ways, through the workshop years by hiring and bonding with people who have become life-long friends. Eventually I just wanted to paint and sell my art so I stopped teaching workshops and I had more time to create. I opened my own gallery on the Mediterranean in Collioure, a town made famous by Matisse and the Fauves. My old fisherman's house was a derelict hovel – but it was on my favorite walking street where all the galleries are, so "Remi, the magnificent", (husband to Nese, our workshop chef) brought his crew, and out of nothing emerged a gallery and two rental apartments.

My favorite joy in life is to be painting in my studio over the gallery and have Cecilia (a French painter who helps me run my gallery L'Art Vivant) send a client up who has a special commission or request. And in the next week while they are in Collioure vacationing, I complete their personal painting. I've realized over and over that it's not as much about the money as it is about making a deep personal offering and connecting in a meaningful way. To spread light and passion and feed the spirit is, hopefully why we all exist.

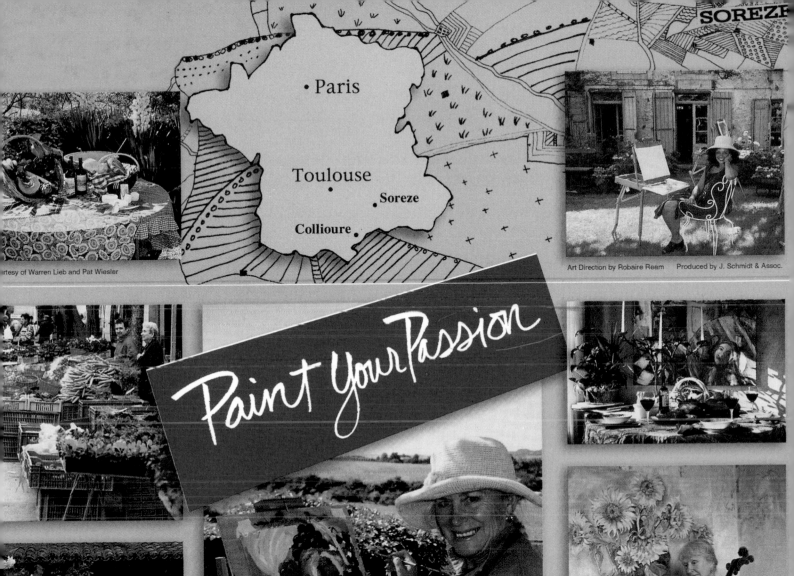

SOREZE

• Paris

Toulouse
• Soreze

Collioure •

...rtesy of Warren Lieb and Pat Wiesler

Art Direction by Robaire Ream   Produced by J. Schmidt & Assoc.

Paint Your Passion

Melting down, searching for intuitive brush strokes, squeezing passion out of paint tubes, inhaling the sea air and dipping in the Mediterranean see-sea. I know why Matisse and the Fauves made major historical leaps here.

Collioure

COLLIOURE

Carole paints and directs her own Gallery l'Art Vivant in the Mediterranean town of Collioure. Fauvism was born here with the vibrant palettes of Henri Matisse and André Derain.

France has been a magnificent teacher for me. I went there to heal my body and reclaim my place as a painter and ended up delving into my French roots and discovering whole villages that practiced my concept of LiveArt without even knowing it. Everywhere I looked, I saw future paintings of simple soul-filled everyday scenes. My village of Soreze was quieter than usual when I first discovered it because a huge boarding school for 500 boys had recently closed. The mayor was wondering what to do with the amazing ballrooms complete with marble fireplaces, parade grounds and magnificent courtyards, the ancient chapel and soaring chestnut groves. The school began in 1164 as an Abbaye and had been the center of the village since Soreze began. I passed on the visionary ideas of Anne Howel for the Ft. Mason Creative Arts Center in San Francisco to the mayor and have had the satisfaction of watching the cultural face-lifting of the old Abbaye as it has evolved into a conference center with a great hotel, restaurant and lots of visiting performing groups, including theater, opera and symphonies.

During the transforming work on the Abbaye, I was doing my own renovations on three 400-year old stone town houses that became the home of my summer painting workshops.

85

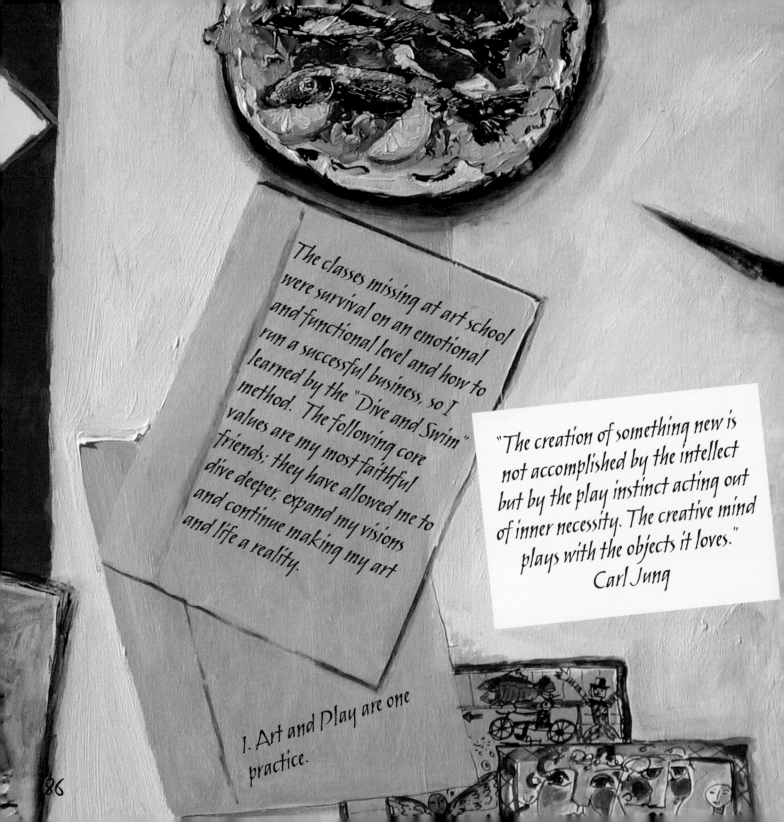

The classes missing at art school were survival on an emotional and functional level and how to run a successful business, so I learned by the "Dive and Swim" method. The following core values are my most faithful friends; they have allowed me to dive deeper, expand my visions and continue making my art and life a reality.

1. Art and Play are one practice.

"The creation of something new is not accomplished by the intellect but by the play instinct acting out of inner necessity. The creative mind plays with the objects it loves."
Carl Jung

The Core Values of Art

1. Art and play are the same practice.
2. Art is Life - Life is Art. Create the type that makes you deeply happy.
3. To succeed, allow difficulties to grow and change into self-directed persistence by watering your own root. Persistence is the key to success. Your only job is to remain engaged in creative work.
4. Master self doubt. It is the only force that can keep you imprisoned. There is never a right way to do art.
5. Begin again. The magic gifts of your creative output await you and the world. Imagine if VanGogh would have given up.
6. Just paint. Everything you need will follow. Markets always exist and pay well for truthful art from your heart. Believe me!
7. Practice stepping away and seeing from every possible angle and perspective. This is where you will find the freedom to grow. Try to suspend time. Develop self-compassion.
8. Find mentors who can't possibly teach you what they know in your lifetime and spend infinite time by their sides. Encouragement is the key.

Creativity lifts you out of difficulties, over the edge of fear and on to the wild ride of new possibilities. Hosting painting adventures in France allowed me to re-define my art identity immensely. I was privileged to paint alongside my mentor and friend, Gregory Kondos, who showed all of us his amazing way with an "essentialists" approach to art and the French countryside. Gregory is definitely a painter's painter. To watch him demonstrate how to find the essence of whatever he paints is astonishing. At one point he advised me to leave out 75% to expand the power in my work. This single comment helped me, puzzled me (but which 75%?), challenged me and moved me along. It's an amazing mentor who can give you the needed 'kick in the pants' and still remain the shining star that they are in your eyes. Gregory is that precious being.

The best surprise outcome evolved while Moni (Greg's wife) and he were in Soreze. We had all spent a painting day at Sabine's old farmhouse (the same one that brought me to Soreze originally), and the Kondo's ended up buying it. Now when I return, my Art family is an integral part of my French dream.

Gregory Kondos (Copyright 2000
French Farm House
Oil on canvas, 30" x 36"

89

Chapter
Seven

Turning Fear
Into Passion

Passion into Paint

COURTESY OF WARREN LIEB

Clockwise from top: Artist Carole Watanabe creates environments at her villa in France, like this one of her courtyard, and then paints them. The guest rooms are decorated in honor of French artists, such as the colorful Matisse Room and the Chagall Room that features a dramatic wall sconce. A retreat participant prepares her paints.

By JUDY HAMMOND
Herald Staff Writer

Painter Carole Watanabe was drawn to the sun-drenched golden fields of southern France. Here she was able to fulfill a passion to paint and teach others to live their life as art.

In an ever-changing landscape of sunflowers and lavender near the village of Soreze, Watanabe thrived in the healing atmosphere of light and color.

"Art comes out of the way we live," said Watanabe in a phone interview from her home in Sebastopol on the eve of her departure for Soreze. "That's why so much beautiful art comes out of southern France."

When Watanabe, 54, discovered the village of Soreze, just 45 minutes from the Mediterranean, she was recovering from a third bout of Lyme disease. At that point, she did not know whether she would recover from the disease, which she contracted from deer ticks on her property near Sebastopol.

"I decided I want to paint in beautiful places the rest of my life," she said.

The pursuit of this dream led her to France. Watanabe and her husband, Don, a builder, bought and restored a small 400-year-old townhouse in the village of Soreze where she could paint and restore her health. She opened her pretty house, which she calls *Villette Live Art,* as an artists' retreat and studio.

Global Live Art, patterned after the art program they founded in Sebastopol in 1994, was on its way in France.

Before too long, the centuries-old large villa across the street began to distract her. "It was an eyesore," she said. Perhaps she could convince the owner to at least paint it. Instead, he suggested that she buy it.

With eight bedrooms and five fireplaces, the villa would accommodate her students more comfortably, and the barn would make an ideal studio with its view of an ancient garden and local bell tower.

"I just fell in love with the house," she said. "We had a lot of friends who had been wanting to come. If they would help us fix it up, they could stay free for a month."

Plumbers, sheetrock installers and others joined the work party. The bedrooms, four of which have fireplaces, are each decorated in the style of a French artist, such as Matisse, Van Gogh, Chagall and Bonnard. The idea is to give the guest the feeling of living in a painting.

The house was given the name, *L'Art Vivant,* or living art.

Every summer the Watanabes open their secluded Soreze homes to students who want an idyllic retreat to explore their creativity, whether it be art,

Please see **Passion into Paint** *page E6*

You can't afford the Fear

Art is a direct route to passion. Through Art you reveal your true self — the gifts you were born to give to the world. Art is healing to the soul; Art makes life visible; Art shines a light into the dark side so you can know that which cannot be accessed in any other way. Art is a truth river in flood stage. Art is more than the painting on the wall, it is the way you live your life, the garden you plant, the quality of your relationships, the way dinner looks on the table.

Creating passion in your life is probably the best gift you will ever give yourself. Passion is infectious and motivating. It inspires you to jump lightly from your bed in the morning and to lie down at night with a feeling of fullness.

94

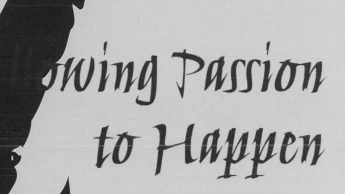llowing Passion to Happen

Passion tickles your body inside and out.

Passion is infectious, overflowing with delight.

Passion is the rocket fuel needed to live the dreams of your aliveness.

When you are being purely passionate, the need to try dies and acceptance takes its place.

When you are being purely passionate, there are no wide separations between your wants, your dreams and reality.

When your passion is truly alive, life's surroundings look like the postcards and the paintings you love.

When passion is in full force, Bliss & Centeredness and Art & Life are married.

When passion reigns and guides the spirit, "Yes" replaces the "But".

When your passion and work merge, you'll be living with the people you love and doing the work that keeps you happy.

Chapter
Eight

Reconstitute
Your Attitudes

Watanabe

Suzuki Roshi at San Francisco Zen Center was asked,

"What is Nirvana?",

he replied,

"Seeing one thing through to the End".

Reconstitute Your Attitudes

When I read my past journals, I realize nothing is ever lost. The skills gained at every phase, every misjudgment, every triumph of new experience are the under-paintings for NOW TIME. They are the rich patinas that give depth and richness to all future phases. We are continuously creating sequels and chapter headings for our life's tale. Hopefully, seeing our art "through to the end" will be the final chapter in a creator's life. Our art work mirrors our moods and the quality of life we are engaged in. In the words of my friend and mentor, Kaz Tanahashi, "You can't hide anything in a line."

As creative beings, we can't afford to wait for inspiration; we need to enter a familiar zone daily where we can call in our creative muse. For me, it happens when I rock in my chair in front of my studio shrine and rearrange the words, flowers, symbols of NOW, light incense, and say some silent power prayers.

Creative juice is your money in the bank, engaged attitudes are your retirement plan. Your support system, love and daily creative work are the automatic deposits to keep your art ship not only floating but exploring new worlds and more profound levels of your art and consciousness.

just a dabbler

I'm no good

have to suffer

I'm not creative

have to be crazy

it's not important

can't make a living

can't draw a straight line

Breaking Through the Road Blocks to Your Expression

But first you'll have to clear the yellow post-its covering your mirror and distorting your identity – the myths of being an artist that don't work.

"The crazier I am the better my work will be and the more respect I'll earn. True Artists are incapable of being true business people. In fact, if my checkbook is balanced and my desk in order and my biz plan clearly written on the wall – I'll probably fail as an artist."

In Art there are no right ways – there is your way, period. Right ways are merely more limits and illusions to get stuck in. Art is a continual re-invention of self – no one escapes. The true joy of the Art Life or LiveArt is that what comes next is always a surprise because there is nothing fixed except your own neuroses. You are not in control.

You do need a cheering section for all your new steps – how can you create and take risks (which always creates change) when the status quo keep voicing fears that attempt to immobilize your sprouting.

Make a life long pact with your most adventurous friends to support and accept you (no matter what). This demands unconditional love which takes some inner spiritual work. True acknowledgement, remembering the good times, and forgiveness: these are the keys to future growth that defies the familiar.

little sardine

continuously begin again..

dive
faith

a fully engaged Tuna

Watanabe

I Am Making This Book

to help expand the oceans of creative juice. No matter where you sit on the creative beach, a beginning sardine, a fully engaged tuna, a burnt-out land locked salmon, or a huge successful name brand marlin - the creative ebb and flow demands that you continuously 'begin again'.

And how will I start over when I'm tired and disappointed? There are so many traps to fall into during transition times, and creative blocks:

- I'm not famous yet and I should be
- My art isn't selling so no reason to make more
- If the world can't recognize my art as great, screw'em.
- My parents still think I'm waiting to find myself - can't they see this life is vital to me?
- I'm sick of being abused by galleries, why bother finding new ones?

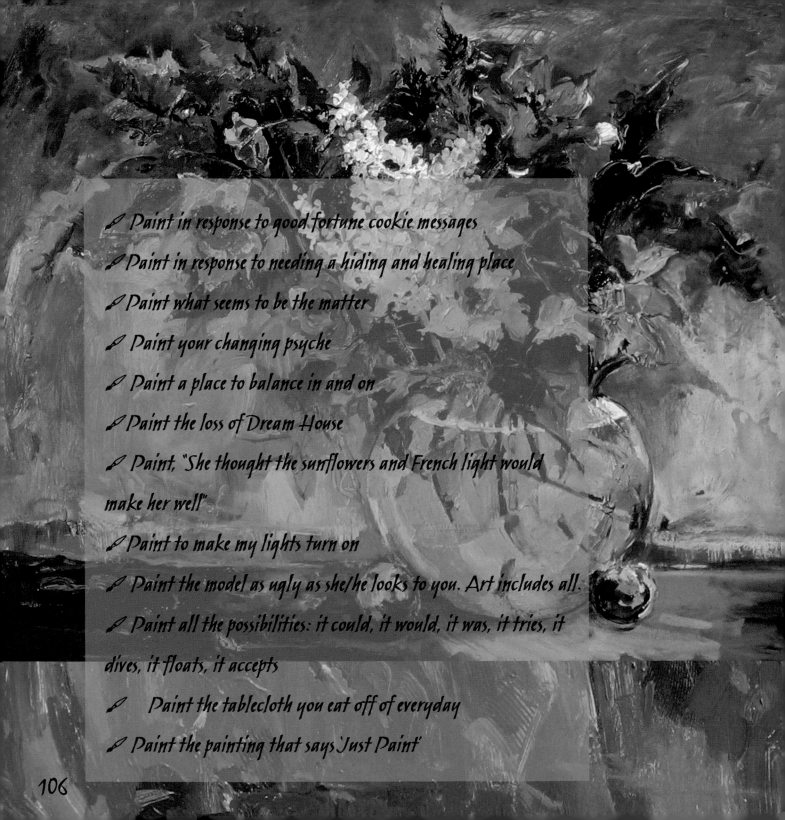

✐ Paint in response to good fortune cookie messages

✐ Paint in response to needing a hiding and healing place

✐ Paint what seems to be the matter

✐ Paint your changing psyche

✐ Paint a place to balance in and on

✐ Paint the loss of Dream House

✐ Paint, "She thought the sunflowers and French light would make her well"

✐ Paint to make my lights turn on

✐ Paint the model as ugly as she/he looks to you. Art includes all.

✐ Paint all the possibilities: it could, it would, it was, it tries, it dives, it floats, it accepts

✐ Paint the tablecloth you eat off of everyday

✐ Paint the painting that says "Just Paint"

Without growth, creativity dies and art becomes an ordinary job - the job of filling orders, doing the bookkeeping and paying for your life of boredom and ease. I arrived there - I could no longer sell my own work because my excitement vanished and the world knew I was trying without self-belief. At that juncture, I wanted to escape San Francisco and the art scene I saw as a brick wall that I was tired of trying to climb. My level of success hadn't met my expectations.

Art is not about trying. Art is an inner force that becomes an addiction. Periodically art about Death is the most vital act you can initiate - make a coffin and bury the art you are bored with and begin to experiment with new media or directions   take classes   become an apprentice - travel to a new culture - learn a new way to speak - gather in the pieces that will make your new puzzle richer and totally engrossing once again..

Painting is a metaphor for life - you create the problems that only you can solve and you spend big time (like your life) solving them to the best of your ability. And if you are willing to destroy and allow chaos on the canvas - magic will smile on you and point the way towards the next thrill on the art trail.

Art is the lamp post with a brightly shining lantern at the end of the tunnel, helping you find your way whether you've paid the electric bill or not. Art leaves no one out. Remember what a joy it was in kindergarten? That joy comes from the inside out and you can always return to it. It demands your compassion for the small hand within that loves to paint and make beauty. Real joy in art demands that you accept your perceived shortcomings, and you continue to begin again and again.

In Matters Of the Mindful Art Spirit

Creative awakening has nothing to do with getting to a place, or accomplishing something, or changing to be better – it's just learning to live and love what you do in this moment and immersing yourself in a process of self-discovery as you swim in your internal universe.

If you could simply love the practice of doing art and live without always measuring yourself against goals, standards, other people, money collected, etc. – if you could simply remain in the present with your whole heart engaged in whatever is happening – you would find that love is what is happening. Making art can allow the mind's chatter to soften and even vanish because Art is about solving very specific problems that only you can make and only you have the mindfulness to solve.

Art Heaven

is an insurance policy against troubles in the bigger world, 9-11 to be exact.

It's a Living Shrine – filled with the best friends a painter could have.

Inside is a juicy place – where the creative urges are encouraged and the Life Force is free to flow in any way it wants.

Art Heaven continues to feed our Sense of Magic as it births new dreams for whoever comes through our doors. We acknowledge the joy and camaraderie, knowing how truly blessed we are.

<u>Just Paint</u> for your own well being, for joy.

Creating Worlds That Nurture Your Creative Fire

The Art world can feel lonesome, difficult and exclusive at times - especially if you haven't become a name brand artist. Since art is how I spend most days, other like-minds for feedback, inspiration and plain old information gathering and problem solving are a necessity.

Creating organizations, camps, clubs, networks are my answer to not liking to feel left out. My most recent support system is Art Heaven, founded as a response to the September 11, 2001 tragedy. During that dark time, creating a place to expand the beauty in our world seemed like the most vital healing balm I could offer to myself and my town of Sebastopol, California. Many friends pulled together to support this idea by purchasing my paintings, my art trips to France and memberships in Art Heaven, etc. until the funds were gathered to purchase our new
Art Heaven/Art House in Sebastopol.

We filled the rooms with easels, work tables, still-life props and most important – a group of people who wanted to paint together. We were open 24/7 as all members had keys and soon the floors looked like a Jackson Pollock painting. Our practice was holistic, we created paintings, created community, created a venue to show and sell our works, gave each other the support and compassion necessary for all types of painters to flourish.

Eventually, after being open to the public for three years, a cohesive group of 10 painters bonded and became invaluable to each others' process. Simultaneously, I (who had been teaching the group) decided to change my role from mentor to guiding light and hostess. I moved the group to my own newly expanded home-studio where painting sessions are still very alive and well. The group of 10 is individuating now and beginning to have shows of their own, expanding the bright and beautiful spots we focus on in our worlds.

This painting honors Juliette Ideler White, my role model and the muse of Art Heaven, who at age 86 is still learning new languages, traveling the world, helping me host painters in San Miguel de Allende and remaining constant and true.
Juliette is a Master of Life.

Art is my spiritual practice Art Heaven is my church, my temple. My art sisters are my creative community - Sarita

Painting brings out the quiet from within. To paint is to go deep, to explore, to gather with like-minded women takes this even further. Love, Color, Dimensions open in this collective gathering - Susan

Art Heaven - it is Heaven to come together with friends and paint our Hearts -

My creative process has been exponentially enhanced by participating in Art Heaven. We have discovered an elegant and loving way to be and to paint together -

Painting opens me to looking, observing what is all around me -

To just be and just paint with all of you is the exact nurturing I need. Thank you for your wonderful energy - Art Love, Carole

I walk up the stone driveway and enter into a sacred circle of strong dynamic women who are busy embracing their lives by creating Art and supporting each other in their individual life's journeys. We all sense our true strength and our connectedness. This is where we are deeply known and feel safe. Laughing with life, we create Art together - Bonnie

Art Heaven is the most valued art community I have created so far. When I'm traveling on vacations, it is the part of my life that I really miss. The stories and deep laughter and satisfaction at seeing so much rich art being created weekly in my studio is immensely fulfilling. If you do art, you might want to make your own Art Heaven. The nuts and bolts are: members pay a monthly fee for a space and lunch. I make soup and provide the space – they bring salad, etc. and their serious intentions to improve their Art practice. We arrange shows, sales, parties, art field trips and even a trip to my house and studio in Mexico yearly as a gift in appreciation for our incredibly valuable creative symbiosis. We pollinate each other without even trying. Please see my website – www.artfully.com – for a "How to create your own Art Heaven" article.

Watanabe

114

The Art Garden is a journal excerpt:

Your Art Garden

Your art is an immense sacred garden
You have the only key
The key is stored in your heart and soul
To truly enter, you must risk immersion, addiction and obsession
The pathways are spiritual in nature
There is no right way – all paths lead to bliss
Persistence is the practice that works
Learning to quiet your fear is the ultimate challenge
Your fears are the crab grass that can choke every flower you try to paint
Just speak firmly to your fears – when you hear their voices, say this mantra:
Thank you first grade teacher
Thank you best friend
Thank you art school…etc
But there is no place for you in this garden.
Know deeply that you are the only boss on this white canvas.
It doesn't matter what you paint
All that counts is how often you show up.
Art is the deepest true love that can be cultivated - the way to private inner happiness
Keeping your art spirit happy is your life's work
Without deep creative bliss, the outer world seems like a job
Your birthright is to create beauty; no one else can do it for you
Every expression of your soul helps to balance the world's negativity
Art is love, you are LIVEART

- Trust whatever gives you the deepest meaning as your art guide and your soul's best friend.

- The perception of beauty is a moral test.

- Success or failure is temporary, only Art is eternal.

Watanabe

Marriage to my Gift

I have found home
Entered my source
The vigorous vision of the NOW PLACE
Is screaming inside me
Take on your new wings
Fly directly to the cleansing temple
Where snapshots of your soul beg to be released
Quietly, patiently, asking to swim into the clear
Oceans of your deepest creative seas
Take down the cobwebs of memory and myth
Who taught you to survive, to tiptoe, and to be reasonable?
Sculpt these states of longing energy into the
Authentic self who has been terrified
To find her hidden painted voice
Plunge into the dance, the interior landscape
Where no cash registers exist, only intuition perched,
Ready to lift the brush as a sword

No Fear Painting

All <u>fear</u> is:

False
Evidence
Assumed
Real

As soon as you get out of your own way and just let the paint fly, you'll feel the dam of creative juice breaking open - Go too far - When you hear any "No's" surfacing or "I can'ts", just breathe and replace it immediately with:

<u>YES</u>

Yes, I am a painter.
Yes, I love color.
Yes, Artists do have more fun.
Yes, life is too short to keep the lock on my own creative force.
Yes, I'm ready to burst out of the Prison of Normal Living.

118

Temple Maintenance

Write these new words on your walls –
I have enough
I am enough
I don't know
JUST PAINT.

Step up to the Art Heaven within,
sliding into the back rooms
where light blue violet fingers massage
the chartreuse wings of the new molten self.

Drink without apology for the gifts you have received.

Know that the art you create for your own Bliss is exactly
what our world craves.
Yell and scream with ecstatic full conviction
as you marry the gifts that only you can give back to yourself
and humanity.

It's important to hold a changeable vision of where you want your art to take you. When I painted Just Us, I knew my art had taken me to a serene, infinite place – where I could paint and my husband could devote his spirit to his music. Voila! May you too find your way to your personal Art Heaven.

122